CHONK
AND
SMOL

Puppers, Woofers, Floofers and Frens

HarperCollins*Publishers*

HarperCollins*Publishers*
1 London Bridge Street
London SE1 9GF

www.harpercollins.co.uk

HarperCollins*Publishers*
1st Floor, Watermarque Building,
Ringsend Road
Dublin 4, Ireland

First published by HarperCollins*Publishers* 2021

10 9 8 7 6 5 4 3 2 1

Text © HarperCollins*Publishers* 2021

HarperCollinsPublishers asserts the moral right to be identified
as the author of this work

A catalogue record of this book is available from the British Library

ISBN 978-0-00-842111-3

Printed and bound in Latvia

MIX
Paper from
responsible sources
FSC™ C007454

This book is produced from independently certified FSC™ paper
to ensure responsible forest management.

For more information visit: www.harpercollins.co.uk/green

CONTENTS

INTRODUCTION

Once upon a time, we lacked the words we needed to express our emotions about the animals we know and love. We tried, but all we could come up with were phrases like, 'Oh, he's so tiny!' or 'She's such a great big cat!' Something was missing. In short, words failed us. They didn't give us the tools to describe all the intensity of our feelings.

Then the Internet came along and everything changed. We came together, shared photos of our sweet friends and found new words to describe their intense cuteness.

No longer is your cat 'large and fluffy' – she's now a **majestic chonk**. No longer is your dog tiny – he's a **smol boi**, and if he's a dachshund he's a **long boi** too. Now we can celebrate all the quirks and cutenesses of our animal pals using words like **floofer**, **woofer**, **boop**, **blep** and **mlem**. They just feel so right. When you see a smol boi tippy-tap towards you hoping for a snacko and a sweet boop on the nose, you have the exact words you need to describe what's going on. Thank you, Internet – we'd be lost without you.

Prepare yourself for borks, zooms and an almost unbearable level of floofiness, and join us for an adorable adventure into the world of *Chonk and Smol*!

GLOSSARY

Need to know your blep from your mlem, or your boop from your snoot? With our handy list, you'll be heckin smart in no time and ready to snug any floofy frens you meet without doing yourself a frighten!

Absolute unit – an animal whose size commands respect.

Bamboozled – when an animal feels confused; for example, when it catches its own tail and doesn't know what to do next.

Blep/blop – to stick your tongue out a little.

Boof – a low, deep bark.

Boop – to bop something with your nose, or to bop something on the nose.

Bork – a bark.

Borkdrive – running while barking.

Catto – a cat.

Chonk – an animal that is so fat or aggressively fluffy, it is almost majestic (see also *Thicc boi*).

Chungus – another name for a true honk (see *Chonk*).

Cloud – a super-fluffy floofer.

Corgo – a corgi.

Dangler – a tail.

Doggo – a dog.

Doing me a frighten – scaring your doggo.

Floofer – an animal that is fluffy and soft (such as a Samoyed or Pomeranian).

Fren – a friend.

Heckin – very.

Hooman – a human.

Long boi – a long or skinny dog.

Mlem – to stick your tongue out all the way.

Party puggo – a pug with a party hat.

Puggo – a pug.

Pupper – a puppy.

Pupperino – an extra-smol pupper.

Smol – an animal that is so small and cute that you feel compelled to protect it.

Smol boi – a smol friend of any kind.

Snacko – a snack.

Snoot – a nose.

Snug – a hug.

Sploot – when a dog or cat stretches so that their bellies are flat on the ground and their back legs are pointing behind them.

Thicc boi – an animal that's chonky and beautiful (see *Chonk*).

Tippy-tap – to dance with happiness.

Woofer – a big doggo.

Wrinkler – a wrinkled dog, e.g. pug or British bulldog.

Yapper – a smol pupper (see also *Smol boi*).

Zoom – run.

Zoomie – when your doggo is running so fast, it's just a blur.

CHAPTER 1

MLEM OR BLEP?

We've all been there: you're thinking hard (or hardly thinking?) and you suddenly notice your tongue is poking out of your mouth slightly. Whether it's just a tongue-tip (a blep) or the full tongue hanging out (a mlem), when a furry pal does it, it's heckin cute.

Somebody order a **BUNNY-BLEP?**

SUN'S OUT,
tongue's out

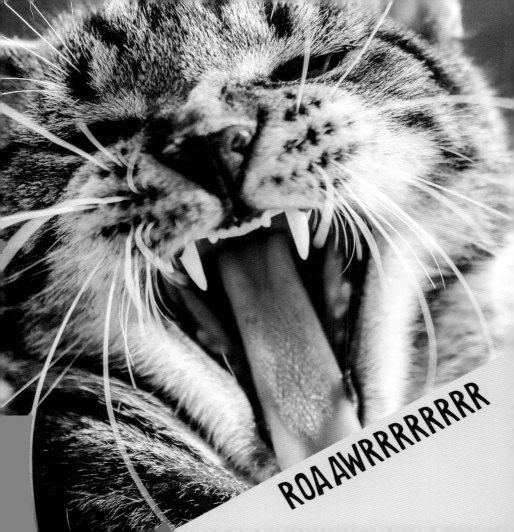
ROAAWRRRRRRR

Water-cooler **MEWMENT**

Happy corgo
BLEP

Let it all **HANG OUT**

FEELIN' BAMBOOZLED:
I ate one, but it disappeared?

I do like to

MLEM

beside the seaside

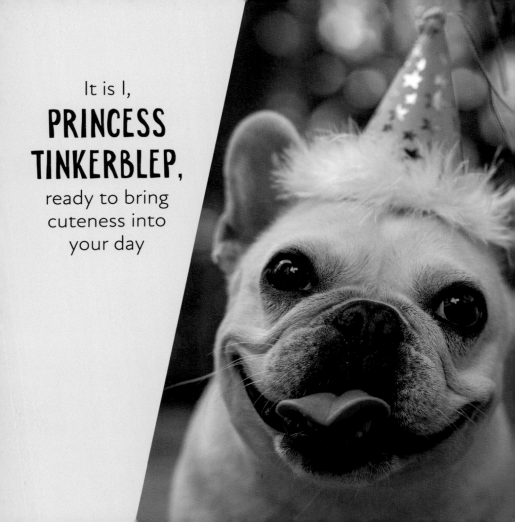

It is I,
PRINCESS TINKERBLEP,
ready to bring
cuteness into
your day

READY OR NOT,
here I mlem!

CHAPTER 2

BORKING

Sometimes a pupper's life suddenly gets heckin EXCITING and before you know it, you're BORKING SUPER-LOUD so everyone can hear! Your owners love to hear it. So do the neighbours! Don't hold back – bork it out loud and clear for everyone to enjoy.

We're going on an
ADVENTURE!
It's
TOP SECRET!

Let's go for a **BORK** in the park

BORKING buddies

I shall now **SING THE SONG** of my people

And liiiiiii-ai-ay will always
BORK YOU-00-00-00-00-00-00

My **BOOFS** go all the way up to 11

HELLO,
up there, will you be my fren?

Just gotta tell everyone
about this amazing
COLD WHITE STUFF!

He may be smol, but this pupperino has **LOTS** to say

Introducing ... **DESTINY'S BORK**

CHAPTER 3

SNUGGING

At the end of a long day's borking and zooming, a floofer needs to rest, and there's no nicer way of doing a snooze than with a furry fren right by your side. Chill out and relax with these snuggly pals.

I gots **DA BEAR** necessities

BFFs

(Basket Frens Furever)

SNOOZLE
with my best fren

Let **SLEEPING CATTOS** lie

I'll keep an **EYE ON THINGS** while you do a snooze

WOOFER FRENS
make the comfiest
pillows

Welcome to our
SLUMBER PARTY

Smol frens,
BIG SNOOZLE

CHAPTER 4

ZOOMING

There's nothing like feeling the wind in your fur and the grass flying under your feet – zooming is one of life's greatest pleasures. You might be chasing a ball or just zooming for the sheer joy of it. Let's go, go, go!

The
BIGGEST ZOOM
starts with a single step

I MAY BE SMOL, but I'm very zoomy

Water-cooled **BORKDRIVE** coming right up!

Nothing gets
between me and
TE ATIME

Even smol
yappers can do
BIG ZOOMIES

Is it a bird? Is it a plane? No, it's **SUPERPUP!**

The **FLOOFIEST OF CLOUDS,** zooming across the snow

Sometimes I like to let my driver do the
ZOOMING FOR ME

CHAPTER 5
BOOPING

Furry pals are so darn
adorable that sometimes
you just have to boop
them – oh so gently –
on their delicate snoots.
And ... boop!

Your boops make me feel **BOUNCY** again

WRINKLY boop, meet **FLOOFY** boop

Brother, won't you **BOOP THIS SNOOT?**

A smol boop makes every day **NICER**

First booping lesson: always be careful which **BIT YOU BOOP**

You wouldn't steal
a boop from a
SNOOZING SMOL BOI ...
would you?

A **BOOPIFUL** moment

A SUNSET
boop to remember

Come closer,
I need to
BOOP YOU

CHAPTER 6
TIPPY-TAPPYING

Life on four legs is great when you're zooming, but sometimes when you're really happy, you can't help but dance on tippy-toes to show the world how you're feeling.

Oh, I do like to **TIPPY-TAP** beside the seaside

Will tippy-tap for

STROKES

The
SNOWFLAKES
up here are even
more refreshing!

A **LITTLE TIPPY-TAP** to see my frens go by

Tippy-tapping
CHEEK TO CHEEK

She jumps, she shoots,
SHE PAWS!

EARS: FLOPPY.
Tippy-tap: adorable

There's nothing this
LONG BOI
can't reach if I try

Are you ready for some advanced-level **TIPPY-TAP?**

CHAPTER 7

DRESSED TO IMPRESS

People are so weird. Even though they know we have our own furry coats, they just love dressing us up in the latest pup couture. I guess we just can't help being floofy style icons. See you on the catwalk!

Tell Santa I've been a very **GOOD BOI** all year

I'm ready for my
CLOSE-UP

They promised I can eat my **CROWN** after the shoot

I'm just happy to **BEE** here

BE AN EWOK, they said. It'll be fun, they said ...

But I thought it was supposed to be **PUSS IN BOOTS**

They call me
PUGGO POTTER

CHAPTER 8

GIVEN A FRIGHTEN

HELP! I just heard something go boop in the night ... Sometimes smol pals and thicc frens get scared and need a warm, soothing paw to make it all better.

If I keep my **EYES CLOSED,** nothing scary can see me

Too much **SCARINESS** for one tiny catto to take!

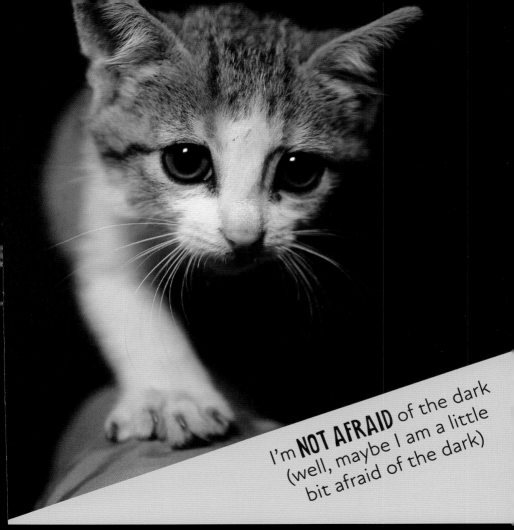

I'm **NOT AFRAID** of the dark
(well, maybe I am a little
bit afraid of the dark)

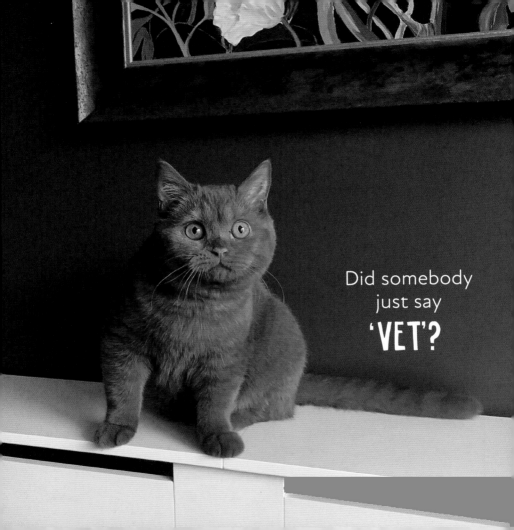

Did somebody just say 'VET'?

I don't think there are monsters UNDER THE BED ...

Startled – *MOI* ?

Tell me
WHEN IT'S SAFE
to come out, pls

It's a **HECKIN** long way down from here ...

You wouldn't give your
BEST PUPPER
a frighten – would you?

Are you sure it's safe to **COME OUT?**

Won't you hold
MY PAW
till I fall asleep?

CHAPTER 9

MAKING FRENS

Life's more fun when you have a fren by your side. We may lead each other into trouble sometimes, but we'll always find an adventure when we're together.

SPLASHY-SPLASH buddies

CLOSE-KNIT frens

Puppy **PALS** forever!

FLOOFY
frens for life

You **HUM IT,** I'll play it

Always take time to stop and **EAT THE FLOWERS**

Wait till you hear what **HAPPENED** next!

We're like **TWO PUPS** in a pod

Dream
A LITTLE DREAM
with me

TOGETHER we can do anything!

CHAPTER 10

AM I HOOMAN

The people we live with have some heckin funny habits. They love staring at those shiny things and they're always talking about something called 'work'. But sometimes I wonder if their way of life is rubbing off on me ...

Puppers need to
relax and recharge too,
YOU KNOW

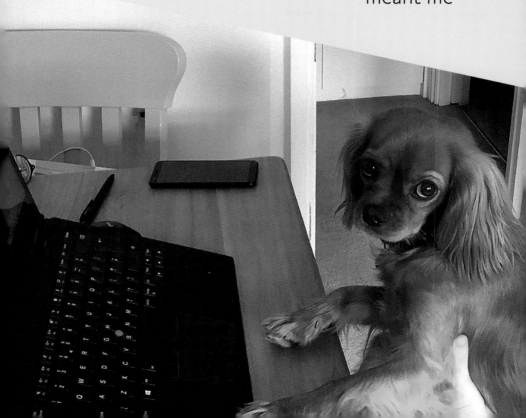

When they said **WORKING LIKE A 'DOG'**, I didn't realise they meant me

Must. Go. To. Bed. Too. Tired. To. **MOVE.**

Time for an
ADVENTURE!
(Please push doggo
for adventure)

So what did she do next? What? No!
OH MY PAWS!

Sealed with a **LICK**

PICTURE CREDITS